Gayle the Goose

Written By: Natasha Peterson
Illustrated by: Witls Games and Animation

www.polarbearpress.com

All rights reserved. No part of this book may be reproduced in any manner whatsoever without written permission, except in the case of brief quotations embodied in critical articles and reviews.

Printed and bound in Canada by: Motion Printing
www.mcp.on.ca

ISBN: 978-0-9952330-0-3

Dedicated to:
Mom, Dad and Grandpa Bert

Gayle the goose was white and was black,
With a long slender neck and two wings on her back.
She had two flat webbed feet, and a tan coloured chest,
She laid eggs in the spring in her low lying nest.
She was a Canada Goose but something was missing,
Her sense of direction left the other geese hissing.

Where am I going? Where is my nest?
Where is the east? And where is the west?
These questions rolled round in her brain all day long.
She couldn't help feeling that she didn't belong.
When out and about did all geese feel muddled?
Gayle wondered if that was the reason they huddled?
When geese fly together in "V" formation,
How does the leader know where to finish migration?

The geese loved routine, they were always the same.
But Gayle was different, they gave her great shame.
Gayle wished she could be just like the rest,
Setting her fears aside, she put her instincts to the test.
She assumed that when leading her gaggle of geese,
Her sense of direction would have to increase.
But at Gayle's turn to lead out the flock,
She was lost after circling the neighborhood block!

Her mistake was too big to hide from the gang,
Who forced her back home like a tossed boomerang.
"We need a new leader, Gayle's always confused."
Their words hurt her deeply, her ego was bruised.
Gayle waddled back to her judgment free nest,
Shed a few tears, and took a small rest.
As Gayle settled down for her much needed nap,
The geese migrated south with their internal map.

But Gayle was forgotten when they all flew away.
And none returned home when they remembered that day.
"She will just slow us down, she does not fit in.
She's missing the compass we all hold within."
They honked in agreement, and continued their quest.
Gayle did not know this was her life changing test.

Gayle frantically fluttered, filled with panic and fear,
As she flew all around, one thing became clear.
She was all on her own, and had nowhere to turn.
Gayle knew it was time to toughen-up and learn.
So she puffed-up her chest, and arched-out her back
I'll fake confidence she thought, who needs a pack?

She started her journey; it was time to begin,
She left Peggy's Cove with all her courage within.
Gayle flew all day, and then flew all night,
She was guided by the colours of the northern lights.

When she finally landed to nibble some flowers,
"Where am I?" she asked, "That's the CN tower."
A pigeon was there to help with her questions.
"How do I go south? Do you have any suggestions?"
"I don't leave the city, just trust your gut.
If you find your way back, you can stay in my hut."
"Thanks", replied Gayle, she was off on her way,
Hoping to find Mexico by end of the day.

When she landed again for a big sip of water,
"That's Niagara Falls" she heard, from an observant otter.
"This place is so beautiful, but it's the wrong way."
"I'm sorry" said the otter, "But please don't dismay.
This is my home, in these fast flowing falls,
If you get lost here, I'll come answer your calls."
"Thanks" replied Gayle, who hopped-up and took flight,
She passed Parliament Hill later that night.

The next time she stopped, she snacked on duckweed,
And amazingly landed at the Calgary Stampede.
What an adventure and my flock's missing it all,
Although all on her own, she no longer felt small.
Gayle's confidence had grown, and her mind expanded.
It was nice not to do what others commanded.

She flew a bit further before turning round.
When all of a sudden, there was no more ground.
Hills jetted up from the base of the earth,
"It's the Rockies", bleated goat admiring its girth.
"Wow" replied Gayle, it was all so new,
"Canada is filled with the most spectacular views."

She flew back to the Cove with nothing to fear.
She no longer felt lost, landmarks made travelling clear.
She dived and she dipped, she danced and she flipped
When flying back home, she was so grateful for this trip.

Her family had already migrated back,
They were all filled with guilt for their verbal attack.
Her flock didn't realize they gave Gayle a gift,
Being thrown to the world gave her confidence a lift.
She learned she did not need her flock to survive,
When all on her own, she could easily thrive.
She was no longer worried about fitting in.
When they heard her adventures, it made the geese grin.

The next year when it was time to migrate away,
It was Gayle's turn to lead south, and she did it her way!
The geese did not know where they would land,
But they knew they loved Gayle and would not disband.

When the geese noticed that Gayle was all turned around,
No bird honked a peep, no one ran her aground.
That winter instead of settling-in somewhere hot,
The geese flew to the North Pole and saw Santa a lot.
Being different was good, even if it seemed strange.
The geese loved Gayle's leading, and welcomed some change.